First World War
and Army of Occupation
War Diary
France, Belgium and Germany

29 DIVISION
Divisional Troops
132 Brigade Royal Field Artillery
1 March 1916 - 12 September 1916

WO95/2292/1

The Naval & Military Press Ltd
www.nmarchive.com
Published in association with The National Archives

Published by

The Naval & Military Press Ltd

Unit 10 Ridgewood Industrial Park,

Uckfield, East Sussex,

TN22 5QE England

Tel: +44 (0) 1825 749494

www.naval-military-press.com

www.nmarchive.com

This diary has been reprinted in facsimile from the original. Any imperfections are inevitably reproduced and the quality may fall short of modern type and cartographic standards.

© **Crown Copyright**
Images reproduced by permission of The National Archives, London, England, 2015.

Contents

Document type	Place/Title	Date From	Date To
Heading	WO95/2292/1 132 Brigade Royal Field Artillery		
Heading	29th Division Divl Artillery 132nd Bde R.F.A. Mar 1916-Sep 1916 Late 57 (How) Bde Bde Broken UA 12.9.16		
Heading	??		
Heading	War Diary of 132 (How) Bde. R.F.A. March 1916 Vol I		
War Diary	Metras Camp	01/03/1916	01/03/1916
War Diary	Alexandria	01/03/1916	13/03/1916
War Diary	Marseilles	15/03/1916	18/03/1916
War Diary	Pont Remy	18/03/1916	29/03/1916
War Diary	Domart-en-Ponthieu	30/03/1916	31/03/1916
Heading	29th Division. 132nd Howitzer Brigade R.F.A. April 1916		
Heading	War Diary of 132nd (How.) Bde R.F.A. April 1916		
War Diary	Domart-en-Ponthieu	01/04/1916	09/04/1916
War Diary	Amplier	09/04/1916	13/04/1916
War Diary	Mailly Maillet	14/04/1916	26/04/1916
War Diary	Englebelmer	27/04/1916	30/04/1916
Heading	29th Division 132nd Howitzer Brigade R.F.A. May 1916		
War Diary	War Diary of 132nd (How) Bde R.F.A. May 1916		
War Diary	Englebelmer	01/05/1916	31/05/1916
Heading	29th Division. 132nd Howitzer Brigade R.F.A. June 1916		
Heading	War Diary of 132nd Bde R.F.A. From 1st June 1916 To 30th June 1916		
War Diary	Englebelmer	01/06/1916	25/06/1916
War Diary	Mailly-Maillet	26/05/1916	30/06/1916
Heading	29th Division 132nd Howitzer Brigade R.F.A. July 1916		
Heading	War Diary of 132nd R.F.A. From 1st To 31st July 1916		
War Diary	Mailly-Maillet	01/07/1916	31/07/1916
Heading	29th Division 132nd Howitzer Brigade R.F.A. August 1916		
Heading	War Diary of 132nd Bde R F A From 1st-31st August 1916		
War Diary	Englebelmer	01/08/1916	31/08/1916
Heading	29th Division 132nd Howitzer Brigade R.F.A. September 1916 Brigade Was Broken Up 12.9.16		
Miscellaneous	D.A.G. 3rd Echelon Base.	25/11/1916	25/11/1916
Heading	War Diary of 132nd Bde R.F.A. Sept 1st-30th 1916 Volume No. 14		
War Diary		01/09/1916	12/09/1916

WO95/2292/1

32 Brigade Royal Field Artillery

29TH DIVISION
DIVL ARTILLERY

132ND HOWITZER BDE R.F.A.

MAR 1916 – SEP 1916

Late 57 (How) Bde

Bde Broken up 12.9.16

WAR DIARY

OF

132 57TH (How.) Bde. R.F.A.

March 1916

Vol I

March 1916 (Erase heading not required.)

Place	Date	Hour	Summary of Events and Information	Remarks and references to Appendices
METRAS CAMP, ALEXANDRIA	1.3.16		The Brigade continues their refitting.	1/C
	2.3.16	About 7.30 p.m.	a message was received to the effect that the 460th Battery R.F.A. was to join the Bde. from Suez, arriving at 12.30 a.m. on 3-3-16. 5 O.R. of R.A.M.C. joined up.	1/C
	3.3.16		The 460th (How.) Battery arrived in Camp at 5.30 a.m — 6 officers and 158 other ranks with 4 guns, 12 wagons, telephone wagon and G.S. Wagon. The officers accompanying the unit were MAJOR S.H. GIBBON R.F.A., LIEUT M. STAVELEY R.F.A., 2Lt J. STEWART R.F.A., 2Lt C.P. DUFF R.F.A., LT H.R. EMERY R.F.A., LT A.S. PHILLIPS R.F.A., CAPT. J. ARMSTRONG A.V.C. joined the Brigade. Orders were received from 29 Div. Arty. re horses and 1st Line Transport, in case unit moved.	1/C
	4.3.16		2Lt W. JOYNSON with 35 O.R. left at 6.50 p.m. for embarkation on H.T. "MANITOU" at PORT SAID - advance party. Scale of ammunition as 4 H.E. to 1 Shrapnel was authorised.	1/C
	5.3.16		2Lt H.R. EMERY was ordered to report to D.A.G., 3rd Echelon.	1/C
	6.3.16		Harness for spare horses (saddlery for artillery) overdrawn. A loan of 10 Chargers and 24 Draught horses was given by 44th Remount Squadron. A new establishment of animals was sent — 34 Chargers, 131 Riding and 393 Draught. Overdrawn were (saddlery) for harness & saddlery (overdrawn) for these.	1/C
	7.3.16		29th Div. Arty. inquired how many supernumerary officers the O.C. wished to retain; the reply was that the O.C. wished to take them all with the Brigade. D.A.Q.M.G. made inquiries as to how many animals per should have ready to embark on the 9th.	1/C
	8.3.16		Orders were received for 13 officers, 215 other ranks and 320 horses with all the vehicles to embark on H.T. "KARSA" at Quay 77 on 9-3-16 at 10 a.m. The 44th Remount Squadron supplied 72 mules for the R.A. 6; and 132 Riding and 156 Draught Horses were received from Cairo. The arrangements for embarkation were that of Bde. H.d. Quarters, A/57, Leo 20, D/57 Leo 20, 5 guns, 9 men of 460th Battery and Bde. Ammn Col., Complete.	1/C

Place	Date	Hour	Summary of Events and Information	Remarks and references to Appendices
ALEXANDRIA	8.3.16 (contd.)		Orders were received today to the effect that the Brigade was to be changed to the 132nd (How.) Bde. R.F.A. and the Batteries Classified as follows — 460th Bty A/132, A/57 B/132, D/57 C/132.	1/C
	9.3.16		The embarkation party moved off shortly after 8 a.m. - Teams and motor lorries being provided: the officers embarking were Headquarters 2Lt H.B.THOMPSON, CAPT I. ARMSTRONG, A.V.C.: A/57 CAPT J.W. MARSDEN, Lt H.O. HOLMES, 2Lt F.O. BAIN, Lt T.G. LOCKWOOD; D/57 MAJOR P.A. MELDON, Lt A.E. HAYNES, 2Lt B. DARLEY, 2Lt J. MORRICE; Pole Ob. Lt C.E.N. GRAHAM, Lt A.S. PHILLIPS, 2Lt D.G. THOMAS. Altogether there were 215 other ranks, 8 chargers, 92 Riding Horses and 148 Draught Horses and 72 mules, 12 guns, 36 ammunition wagons and 1 Telephone Cart embarked.	1/C
	10.3.16		Information came that the rest of the Brigade would embark on the ELELE on 11-3-16. Orders re embarkation amended — only eight officers to embark ELELE, whilst the other three would join the 747th Battery R.F.A. H.T. KAROA sailed.	1/C
	11.3.16		The remainder of the Bde embarked — HeadQuarters Lt. Col H.W. MARRIOTT-SMITH, LT. T.I. CUNNISON, CAPT. J.P. ALLIN R.A.M.C. L A/132 MAJOR T.H. GIBBON, LT M. STAVELEY, LT C.P. DUFF, 2Lt S. STEWART and 2Lt J.C. LISTER (temporarily attached from C/132) and 203 other ranks with 230 horses and mules. H.T. ELELE sailed at 6.30 p.m.	1/C
	13.3.16		Lts. H.M. SIMMS, T. HUTTON, R.E.R. WEBSTER sailed for MARSEILLES along with part of 147th Bde R.F.A.	1/C
MARSEILLES	15.3.16		KAROA arrived at MARSEILLES.	1/C
	16.3.16		First contingent left MARSEILLES in two trains.	1/C
	18.3.16		ELELE arrived at MARSEILLES and Second Contingent left in two trains.	1/C

and the Staff Manual respectively. Title Pages
will be prepared in manuscript.

(Erase heading not required.)

Place	Date	Hour	Summary of Events and Information	Remarks and references to Appendices
PONT REMY	18.3.16		The first contingent arrived and moved into billets.	1/c
	19.3.16		LT-COL H.W.M. SMITH R.F.A. arrived; he took over post of Commandant at PORT REMY.	1/c
	20.3.16		A/132 arrived and moved into billets.	1/c
	21.3.16		Remainder of Bde arrived – Headquarters of the Bde were fixed up at The CHATEAU, PORT REMY. LT H.O. HOLMES proceeded to DUBLIN on leave.	1/c
	22.3.16		All the units were busily engaged with their teams – as there are 101 mules attached and the Bde is 85 drivers short, there is a big strain on the units in getting out the teams. LT A.E. HAYNES and LT C.P. DUFF proceeded to ENGLAND on leave. Owing to no forage having arrived on 21.3.16, its units were very short – fortunately the Supply Officer at ABBEVILLE, who is not the Bde Supply Officer, rendered assistance by despatching 1 ton of hay & ½ton of oats. The deficient forage arrived from AILLY from the Bde Supply section. 29th Div. ArtY. HeadQtrs, who came on 21.3.16, took up their position in the Chateau at COCQUEREL.	1/c
	23.3.16		LT C.E.V. GRAHAM and LT D.G. THOMAS proceeded on leave. leave stopped. The weather was very bad today and the horse lines are getting very muddy.	1/c
	24.3.16		A draft of 87 other ranks joined the Bde today	1/c

(Erase heading not required.)

Place	Date	Hour	Summary of Events and Information	Remarks and references to Appendices
PONT REMY	25.3.16		The bad weather continued and there was a fall of snow, which however melted quickly. A/132 and B/132 moved their horse lines.	1/C
	26.3.16		The men were given as easy a day as possible; in the evening a service was held, conducted by the 29 Div. Arty. Chaplain.	1/C
	27.3.16		In the morning the O.C. inspected all the units on Marching Order. Lt STAVELEY and Lt BAIN with 6 other Ranks went on leave. Orders were received for a billeting party to proceed on 28.3.16 to SARTON	1/C
	28.3.16		Lt T.J. CUNNISON with 7 other Ranks left for SARTON; on arrival their orders were received by the billeting party to return to DOMART-en-PONTHIEU, owing to alteration in the Artillery Billeting Area.	1/C
	29.3.16		The Brigade got ready to move.	1/C
DOMART-en-PONTHIEU	30.3.16		Leaving at 0930 the Brigade marched to DOMART-en-PONTHIEU. The horse lines are situated in a meadow in a well sheltered position; as the water is over a mile away, the time for stables is rather drawn out.	1/C
	31.3.16		The usual routine was followed. Headquarters, 29th Div? Arty and the remainder of the Div? Arty. marched into DOMART-en-PONTHIEU today.	1/R

Thos. J. Cunnison
Lt. R.F.A.,
Adjutant 132nd (How.) Bde R.F.A.

29th Division.

132nd HOWITZER BRIGADE

R. F. A.

APRIL 1 9 1 6

INTELLIGENCE SUMMARY

Vol II

WAR DIARY

OF

132nd (How.) Bde R.F.A.

APRIL 1916.

Instructions regarding War Diaries and Intelligence Summaries are contained in F. S. Regs., Part II. and the Staff Manual respectively. Title Pages will be prepared in manuscript.

INTELLIGENCE SUMMARY

(Erase heading not required.)

Place	Date	Hour	Summary of Events and Information	Remarks and references to Appendices
DOMART-en-PONTHIEU	1-4-16		The units of the Brigade went out in Marching Order this forenoon, independently. The remainder of the day was occupied in the usual routine.	J.J.C.
	2-4-16		A Divisional Artillery Church Parade was held in the Brigade Gun Park this morning. Some difficulty arose today in the Evacuation of sick, as there was no field Ambulance near and no arrangements made for the Transport of sick. A draft of 26 other ranks joined today. Orders were received in the early morning for 1 Battery Commander, 1 F.O.O. and 14 other ranks to proceed by motor lorry up to the firing line to be attached to the 31st Div: A/132 provided the party.	J.J.C.
	3-4-16		2 officers of the East Anglian Bde R.F.A. arrived today — they are attached to the Bde temporarily for accommodation and rations.	J.J.C.
	4-4-16		The good weather of the last few days gave way to a cold, misty morning. The batteries carried out their usual programme of training.	J.J.C.
	5-4-16		Today Headquarters and the Right section of A/132 left for ACHEUX — the section went into action near MAILLY-MAILLET taking over the guns of the 31st Division; the wagon line is situated at BEAUSSART. MAJOR P.A. MELDON, commanding C/132, went to hospital with injury to the eye — this was probably a recurrence of the trouble that originates with the shell wound at HELLES. 2.ts. E.E. BARRS, R.F.A. (T) and A. CORBETT, R.F.A. (T), who arrived on 3-4-16 have been attached to B/132 and C/132 respectively.	J.J.C.
	6-4-16		The left section of A/132 went into action today — they also exchanged guns. After the two sections had joined, the Battery was rather badly shelled but there were only two slight casualties; it is not thought, however, that the enemy had found out the position.	J.J.C.

Instructions regarding War Diaries and Intelligence Summaries are contained in F. S. Regs., Part II. and the Staff Manual respectively. Title Pages will be prepared in manuscript.

INTELLIGENCE SUMMARY

(Erase heading not required.)

Place	Date	Hour	Summary of Events and Information	Remarks and references to Appendices
DOMART-en-PONTHIEU	7.4.16		2Lts D.G. THOMAS, J.C. LISTER and H.M. SINNIS with 35 other ranks proceeded to VALHEUREUX on a Convoi of Trench Mortars.	J.C.
	8.4.16		A billeting party left for AMPLIER: this village was very crowded but accommodation was found for the men in huts - the officers also had to sleep in huts.	J.C.
	9.4.16		The Brigade marched to AMPLIER, leaving at 10 a.m. and arriving at 3:30 p.m. On the way into the village Major-General HUNTER-WESTON inspected the Brigade and expressed his great satisfaction at their appearance.	J.C.
AMPLIER	10.4.16		In the same place there are quartered details of the 15th Bde R.H.A gon 7th Bde R.F.A., 147th Bde R.F.A, 132nd Bde R.F.A. less A/132, 31st Divl. Ammn. Col. & Surrey Yeomanry. Six officers with 98 other ranks went up to the line to dig emplacements for the Batteries: they proceeded to Headquarters Divl. Arty. ACHEUX and thence to billets at MAILLY-MAILLET.	J.C.
	11.4.16		The weather broke down rather badly today and rain fell continuously with the result that the huts got very damp. The O.C. Brigade spent today like yesterday up at the front reconnoitring positions - a little confusion arose as the batteries were originally to come under the orders of the left Group Artillery, but the establishment of a Howitzer Group with Lt.Col. H.R.W. MARRIOTT-SMITH R.F.A. in Command solved the difficulty.	J.C.
	12.4.16		Headquarters moved up from AMPLIER to MAILLY-MAILLET: the new position was taken up in a convent, where the 76th Siege Battery were also billeted.	J.C.
	13.4.16		The unsettled weather still continued - B/132 continues their digging but C/132 were unable to start as their position was not fixed.	

Instructions regarding War Diaries and Intelligence Summaries are contained in F.S. Regs., Part II. and the Staff Manual respectively. Title Pages will be prepared in manuscript.

INTELLIGENCE SUMMARY
(Erase heading not required.)

Place	Date	Hour	Summary of Events and Information	Remarks and references to Appendices
MAILLY-MAILLET	14.4.16		The weather improved slightly. As each Battery will be required to cover the whole Divisional Front, it rather seems as if the number of observation stations will be large, because it is impossible to see the whole front from any one place.	J.J.C. Ref. map BEAUMONT 1/10,000.
	15.4.16		There was a continuation of the fine weather. The position of C/132 was finally fixed at Q.21.b.90.40; B/132 and A/132 being at Q.8.b.30.10 and Q.2.c.70.40 respectively.	J.J.C.
	16.4.16		C/132 moved into their new billets at ENGLEBELMER and began their work on the gun emplacements; this was impeded somewhat as two German Balloons were up for a considerable portion of the day. B/132 finished their two emplacements and arranged to occupy them on the night of 17/18. Their wagon line is to be at BETRANCOURT.	J.J.C.
	17.4.16		The weather changed again for the worse, as there were heavy showers all day. B/132 came into position tonight arriving about 21.30	J.J.C.
	18.4.16		A strong wind blew all day and the rain hardly ever stopped. Orders were received today that B/132 must move their wagon lines from BETRANCOURT, as this place is not in 29th DIVISION Area.	J.J.C.
	19.4.16		A very wet forenoon gave way to a dry afternoon. The Zones of the Batteries were allotted as follows – A/132 or H3, 15.14 to 77.47 (Q.10) : B/132 or H2, Q.10.d 55.70 to 77.17(b.b). C/132 or H1, 77.17 to Q.5.c.30.85. The wagon lines of B/132 were moved to BEAUSSART.	J.J.C.
	20.4.16		Special orders were received concerning storage of six days' rations, two days' water and a stock of ammunition near gun emplacements.	J.J.C.

INTELLIGENCE SUMMARY

(Erase heading not required.)

Place	Date	Hour	Summary of Events and Information	Remarks and references to Appendices
MAILLY-MAILLET	20.4.16	(contd)	B/132 registered their reference line on Q.12.a.37.10. Owing to lack of material progress on the emplacements of C/132 was somewhat slow.	T/C
	21.4.16		With the help of aeroplane observation B/132 registered a M.G. Emp¹ Q.10.B.80.90. The pilot and observer discussed the shoot with CAPT. MARSDEN both before and after. Orders came today to the effect that for tactical purposes A/132 was to be attached to Right Group Artillery and B/132 to Left Group.	T/C
	22.4.16		The weather continues very bad. 2nd LT A.CORBETT proceeded on a covered Trench Mortar Bde at K.33.C.80.60. An Observation Post was fixed up today for the O.C. Right Group. A/132 were ordered to register a M.G. Emp¹ at Q.24.b.20.40 with a view to engaging it at night. C/132 came up into position tonight. The infantry carried out a successful raid with Artillery support. A/132 were in action from 21.20 to 21.50, and 6" Howitzers at MAILLY-MAILLET continued the firing from 21.50 to 22.25.	Reference Maps BEAUMONT and HEBUTERNE 1/10,000 T.J.C.
	23.4.16		C/132 began to register – B/132 continues their registration with aeroplane. C/132 were attached to Left Group for tactical Purposes.	T.J.C.
	24.4.16		Brig-Gen M. PEAKE, C.M.G. Comdg. 29th Div Arty. inspected the lines of the Ammunition Column at AMPLIER.	T.J.C.

INTELLIGENCE SUMMARY

(Erase heading not required.)

Instructions regarding War Diaries and Intelligence Summaries are contained in F.S. Regs. Part II and the Staff Manual respectively. Title Pages will be prepared in manuscript.

Place	Date	Hour	Summary of Events and Information	Remarks and references to Appendices
MAILLY-MAILLET	25.4.16		The B.G.,R.A., 29th Division inspected the wagon lines of the Batteries of the Brigade at BEAUSSART and expressed himself as very well pleased with the condition of the horses of A/132; Those of C/132 were in good condition, but as the animals of B/132 were not looking so well, the B.G.,R.A. ordered their lines to be changed.	J.C.
	26.4.16		Orders were received that the Bde Headquarters were to exchange billets with the 147 Bde R.F.A. Headquarters: accordingly, in the afternoon the Bde Staff moves to ENGLEBELMER. Lt-Col. H.R.W. MARRIOTT-SMITH, Comdg. the Bde, proceeded on leave today: MAJOR.I.H.GIBBON R.F.A., A/132 took over command of the Brigade. CAPT. J.R.P.ALLIN, R.A.M.C. also proceeded on leave and was replaced by Lt C.GORDON, R.A.M.C.	J.C.
ENGLEBELMER	27.4.16		The good weather which began two days ago continues; everything was very quiet.	J.C.
	28.4.16		"Lt A.CORBETT returned from course. More timber for emplacements for C/132 was received.	
	29.4.16		Two raids were made this evening - first, on front 20.21, opposite MARY REDAN: our side did not capture any prisoners and as the German Trench had not been completely blown in - second, on N.W. face of HAWTHORN REDOUBT from pt 77.17 Northwards - the German wire was cut and the trenches badly damaged: our raiding party though advancing to some suffered serious loss. The Batteries of the Bde all did good work.	J.C.
	30.4.16		The wagon line of B/132 was moved to AMPLIER — there was a great deal of shooting today at our aeroplanes.	J.C.

Tho J Linnicon L.R.F.A.
Adjutant 132 Bde R.F.A.

29th dDivision

132nd HOWITZER BRIGADE

R. F. A.

M A Y 1 9 1 6

Army Form C. 2118

WAR DIARY
or
INTELLIGENCE SUMMARY
(Erase heading not required.)

Instructions regarding War Diaries and Intelligence Summaries are contained in F. S. Regs., Part II. and the Staff Manual respectively. Title Pages will be prepared in manuscript.

Place	Date	Hour	Summary of Events and Information	Remarks and references to Appendices

War Diary

of

132nd (How.) Bde R.F.A.,

May 1916.

WAR DIARY or INTELLIGENCE SUMMARY

Army Form C. 2118

(Erase heading not required.)

Place	Date	Hour	Summary of Events and Information	Remarks and references to Appendices
ENGLEBELMER	1.5.16		Things were very quiet today.	Reference Map BEAUMONT 1/10000 T/C
	2.5.16		A very heavy thunderstorm took place this afternoon.	T/C
	3.5.16		There is nothing outstanding to note - the Batteries carried on their work of improving their positions.	T/C
	4.5.16		Major J.H. GIBBON, R.F.A. A/132 has been awarded the D.S.O. for his services on the Peninsula. Lt Col H.R.W. MARRIOTT-SMITH, Comdg 132 Bde R.F.A. returned from leave today.	T/C
	5.5.16		Nothing out of the usual occurred today.	T/C
	6.5.16		MAJOR N.H.C. SHERBROOKE arrived to take over command of C/132 vice MAJOR P.A. MELDON, evacuated sick.	T/C
	7.5.16		Lt Col H.R.W.M. SMITH left for FLIXECOURT to attend a course at the FOURTH ARMY INFANTRY SCHOOL: MAJOR SHERBROOKE assumed temporary command of the Brigade. The enemy registered MARY REDAN and the trenches running N. of it during the day; there too were bombarded at night and a raid attempted, but this was unsuccessful.	T/C
	8.5.16		Owing to restrictions on the use of 4.5" Ammunition the Batteries of this Brigade are doing practically no shooting.	T/C
	9.5.16		New orders re War Establishment owing to this role providing the personnel of 1 Medium Trench Mortar Battery (Z.29) were received - 2 Officers and 23 other ranks are to be added to the Establishment. Also, 1 officer 1 Batman and 1 Riding Horse per Battery are also to be added.	T/C

WAR DIARY or INTELLIGENCE SUMMARY

Army Form C. 2118

(Erase heading not required.)

Instructions regarding War Diaries and Intelligence Summaries are contained in F.S. Regs., Part II. and the Staff Manual respectively. Title Pages will be prepared in manuscript.

Place	Date	Hour	Summary of Events and Information	Remarks and references to Appendices
	10.5.16		Fourth Army No. 163 (G.) was received today; this refers to the reorganization of Artillery Brigades – the 132nd Bde. will cease to exist at 6 p.m. on 13.5.16 and the personnel will be transferred to 18pdr Bde Columns.	7.I.C.
	11.5.16		More instructions re reorganization were received.	7.I.C.
	12.5.16		Very quiet – no fresh developments.	n/c
	13.5.16		The transfer of personnel to DAC was completed.	n/c
	14.5.16		Lt Col H R W M SMITH returned from Army HQrs FLIXECOURT.	n/c
	15.5.16		During the night there seemed to be a heavy bombardment going on on the left of our line – hostile – Maillet also came in for some shelling – finally some allied shells – otherwise quiet	JVS J
	16.5.16		Quiet all day	JVS J
	17.5.16		Re organisation of artillery	JVS J
	18.5.16		Englebelmer fairly shelled – 16 betterus in front of E – from 2/pm – 4.30pm a very slow rate fire all the time	JVS J
	19.5.16		Re organisation of 132 Bdr has taken place. The Bdr was awarded of following Bty's – 369", 370", 371" Re organisation	JVS J
	20.5.16		Gylchner Bdr Bty's from 8.30am.	JVS J
	21.5.16		Gylchner again shelled from 8.30am.	JVS J
	22.5.16		No fresh developments to report.	JVS J
	23.5.16		Rained practically all day. Enemy fairly quiet all day	JVS J
	24.5.16		A few shells fell on outskirts of Gylchner doing no damage &	JVS J

WAR DIARY
or
INTELLIGENCE SUMMARY

(Erase heading not required.)

Army Form C. 2118

Place	Date	Hour	Summary of Events and Information	Remarks and references to Appendices
	25/5/16 26/5/16		Enemy more active than usual, mostly trying to find his trenches. Things were quieter again today.	J.J.C. J.J.C.
	27.5.16		There was heavy firing for about ten minutes this evening in the direction of COLIN CAMPS.	J.J.C.
	28.5.16		ACHEUX Wood was shelled this morning.	J.J.C.
	29.5.16		The outskirts of ACHEUX were again shelled this forenoon. The enemy shelled GABION AVENUE, searching along it from about 100 yds from its end to 200 yds in. Several shells fell close to the 370th Battery, but no material damage was done. The open beyond it;	J.J.C.
	30.5.16		The same parts of ACHEUX and GABION AVENUE were shelled again this morning – in addition, the SUCRERIE was also shelled in the forenoon. The enemy were active all day, but quietness down in the evening. 14 other ranks were received from 29th D.A.C.	J.J.C.
	31.5.16		The enemy were quiet today, confining themselves to desultory shelling in the AUCHONVILLERS sector (no changes in the composition of this brigade are here recorded). Originally the 57th Brigade 10th Division it consisted of A B C D howitzer batteries and the ammunition column. B & C Batteries went to France & there to admin. H.Q. A & D went to Seaford Park Bay. Later their horses and drivers @ in England when they were subsequently dis the latest other batteries this part of the bde dismantled. Guns and landed in Keller — own)	J.J.C.

WAR DIARY
or
INTELLIGENCE SUMMARY

(Erase heading not required.)

Army Form C. 2118

Place	Date	Hour	Summary of Events and Information	Remarks and references to Appendices
			After the evacuation of this place proceeded to Egypt. Here they became the 132 Bde with the addition of 460 Bty & joined the 29th Divn. Gto were with us in Divnl instructions. The full establishment of horses were complete in Divnl Ammn prior to embarkation letter on Divns there were one in the young at Alexandria. Drivers after tasting in France 2 weeks elapsed before Ammn Divers came. An Ammunition column was formed. Draun by mules where heights ranged from 16 to 28 hands. This month B & 460 Batteries went to other brigades of the 29th Divn and 369, 370 & 371 Batteries joined the Brigade. The Ammunition column was horsed up and distributed throughout the Divn Ammn Col.	

J. H. Smith
Lt Col R.F.A.
cmdg 132 R.B.C.

29th Division.

132nd HOWITZER BRIGADE

R. F. A.

JUNE 1916

Army Form C. 2118

WAR DIARY
or
INTELLIGENCE SUMMARY

(Erase heading not required.)

Vol 4

Instructions regarding War Diaries and Intelligence Summaries are contained in F. S. Regs., Part II. and the Staff Manual respectively. Title Pages will be prepared in manuscript.

Place	Date	Hour	Summary of Events and Information	Remarks and references to Appendices
			War Diary of 132nd Bde R.F.A. from 1st June 1916 to 30th June 1916.	

Army Form C. 2118

Instructions regarding War Diaries and Intelligence Summaries are contained in F.S. Regs., Part II. and the Staff Manual respectively. Title Pages will be prepared in manuscript.

WAR DIARY
or
INTELLIGENCE SUMMARY
(Erase heading not required.)

Place	Date	Hour	Summary of Events and Information	Remarks and references to Appendices
ENGLEBELMER			June	BEAUMONT 57D. S.E. 1 & 2 1/10,000 and SECRET map Kiama area T.J.C.
	1.6.16		From 0450 to 0645 the end of GABION AVENUE and 370th Bty R.F.A. were shelled by 15cm. howitzer at intervals of a minute; some desultory shelling of the same places took place later on in the morning. One direct hit was obtained on an emplacement and a dug-out was also slightly damaged — there were no casualties in the course of the afternoon: the wire from HeadQto D/132 was cut in about a dozen places. There were no casualties.	
	2.6.16		The enemy were quieter today and there was very little shelling.	
	3.6.16		Throughout the day things were fairly quiet — about midnight we began a bombardment prior to a raid of the enemy's trenches just North of HAWTHORNE REDOUBT, about Q.4.d.8.7.00; when the infantry entered the trenches they found that the enemy had left, but identification was obtained from a document. A raid in the COLINCAMPS Sector was also carried out successfully at the same time.	T.J.C.
	4.6.16		In the Gazette this morning the names of Lt.Col. H.R.W.MARRIOTT SMITH Comdg. 132 Bde R.F.A., MAJOR P.A.MELDON, late C/132 and Lt. C.E.V. GRAHAM late 132 Bde Am. Col. appeared — the first two being awarded the D.S.O. and the third the Military Cross.	T.J.C.
	5.6.16		The enemy were quiet today. After a quiet day our heavy guns began a bombardment about 11 p.m., which lasted for over an hour; the enemy retaliated feebly.	T.J.C.
	6.6.16		The enemy's activity was below normal — he fired a few shrapnel at the road leading from ENGLEBELMER to 371st Batty and wounded one of our working party	T.J.C.

WAR DIARY
or
INTELLIGENCE SUMMARY

(Erase heading not required.)

Army Form C. 2118

Place	Date	Hour	Summary of Events and Information	Remarks and references to Appendices
ENGLEBELMER	7.6.16		Official news was received today about the death of Lord Kitchener. About midday several shrapnel were burst close to ENGLEBELMER but without effect.	J.J.C.
	8.6.16		The order from His Majesty re death of Lord Kitchener was circulated today, as also the reply to the Army's telegram on the occasion of His Majesty's Birthday. The first train load of ammunition came up late tonight; each Battery drawing ammunition from the train sends a party of 15 men to the halting Place and there the ammunition is taken to guns by hand or wagon — the following are the places allotted to the Batteries of this Bde — 369, MAILLY STATION; 370 & 371, Q 15.c. 60.60; D/132, Q.22.a.55.65.	J.J.C.
	9.6.16		The wet weather still continued. The ammn train was unable to run tonight, probably owing to the neighbourhood of MAILLY STATION being heavily shelled.	J.J.C.
	10.6.16		In the early afternoon the enemy shelled the outskirts of ENGLEBELMER, evidently shooting at the battery there. In the evening the guns of 371st Battery were brought into position from AMPLIER; this makes all the guns of the Brigade in action. About 11:30 p.m. a bombardment was opened on our front and support lines at MARY REDAN, a good deal of damage being done: our artillery replied vigorously.	J.J.C.
	11.6.16		There was a continuance of the miserable weather. The batteries began work on their "Battle O.P's"	J.J.C.

Army Form C. 2118

WAR DIARY
or
INTELLIGENCE SUMMARY
(Erase heading not required.)

Instructions regarding War Diaries and Intelligence Summaries are contained in F.S. Regs., Part II. and the Staff Manual respectively. Title Pages will be prepared in manuscript.

Place	Date	Hour	Summary of Events and Information	Remarks and references to Appendices
	12.6.16		Work on the Brigade O.P. in CHARLES AVENUE was begun today. The ammunition supply by tram has been working very successfully, but the Batteries are kept hard at it on the following day storing the ammunition.	J.G.
	13.6.16		The forenoon was wetter even than we have become accustomed to recently. At a conference of Brigade Commanders some announcements were made regarding future plans – as a result all work is being speeded up.	J.G.
	14.6.16		The enemy activity was below normal today.	J.G.C.
	15.6.16		Things were again quiet. Operation Order (29th Division) No. 36 was received.	J.G.
	16.6.16		Orders from Corps and Divisional Artillery arising out of 29th Div. Order No. 36 were received. Lt. Col. H.R.W. MARRIOTT SMITH, D.S.O. Commanding the Brigade will be attached to 88th Infantry Brigade as Liaison Officer.	J.G.C.
	17.6.16		Orders were received concerning (i) the move of the Battery Wagon Lines and (ii) Supply of Ammunition during the Bombardment. The enemy aircraft were busier today than for some time past – at one time three machines were over at once.	J.G.
	18.6.16		The Wagon Lines of 370 and 371 Batteries moved from AMPLIER to LOUVENCOURT. Enemy machines were again across our lines today and strong British squadrons	J.G.C.

Place	Date	Hour	Summary of Events and Information	Remarks and references to Appendices
	19.6.16		went also. Our A.A. guns drove off enemy aeroplanes but two of which were compelled to land in their own lines. The wagon lines of 369 and D/132 Batteries moved from MAILLY and ENGLEBELMER Woods respectively to LOUVENCOURT. The South side of ENGLEBELMER was shelled at irregular intervals by a 20 cm Howitzer — while no damage was done, the shells were falling in the neighbourhood of a 60-Pounder Battery. Some amendments to Operation Order No 36 were received.	J.C. J.J.C.
	20.6.16		The enemy continued to "crump" the S. side of the village — & in the afternoon they fired several rounds Battery Fire at the Heavy Battery, but did little damage, a few rounds of ammunition only being destroyed.	J.C.
	21.6.16		The enemy was very quiet today — in the afternoon an enemy aeroplane was forced to land in his own lines. Some amendments to Div. Arty. Orders consequent on alterations of Operation Order No 36 were received.	J.J.C.
	22.6.16		The inhabitants of ENGLEBELMER were ordered to leave the village.	J.C.
	23.6.16		2ⁿᵈ Lt W.O.H.JOYNSON, D/132 was evacuated sick — 2ⁿᵈ Lt J.C.LISTER, D/132 was transferred to 369 R.F.A. Headquarters were moved today to LOUVENCOURT. There was a very heavy dust storm followed by	

Army Form C. 2118

WAR DIARY
or
INTELLIGENCE SUMMARY
(Erase heading not required.)

Instructions regarding War Diaries and Intelligence Summaries are contained in F. S. Regs., Part II. and the Staff Manual respectively. Title Pages will be prepared in manuscript.

Place	Date	Hour	Summary of Events and Information	Remarks and references to Appendices
	24.5.16		Rain and thunder this afternoon. "U" Day. The Batteries were engaged in wire-cutting. Several prematures from 18pdrs caused casualties - two men of J/32 were injured by one. Owing to the wet weather, ROTTEN ROW was closed to the Convoys of Ammunition at night with the result that they had to make a long detour.	J.G.
	25.5.16		"V". In the early morning we poured gas on the enemy's trenches - the Germans in retaliation shelled MAILLY-MAILLET causing some casualties to the Seaforth Highlanders. The Headquarters office was moved to the billet in MAILLY-MAILLET occupied by 147th Bde R.F.A. The wire cutting continued and the Heavy Artillery were also busy all day. One of the men wounded in J/132 died today.	J.G.
MAILLY-MAILLET	26.5.16		"W". About ten o'clock we liberated gas on the enemy's trenches; in addition to wire cutting there was a short bombardment by all the guns. The villages in the German lines were all dealt with by our Heavy Artillery and Heavy Trench Mortars fired on BEAUMONT HAMEL doing a great deal of damage. Several shells fell in MAILLY-MAILLET during the day and the R.E. Dump of the 4th Divn was set on fire and burnt out. Official confirmation came of the report that three hostile balloons had been brought down by the R.F.C. No. 6798 B.S.M. H. DISLEY of 370th Asty R.F.A. has been appointed 2/Lt., 3 R.F.A. to date from 30.4.16 (List No. 80, 29/4-16)	J.G.
	27.5.16		"X". CAPT. C. G. HETHERINGTON, Commanding 370th By was admitted to Hospital from the effects of a	

1875 Wt. W 503/826 1,000,000 4/15 J.B.C. & A. A.D.S.S./Forms/C. 2118.

WAR DIARY
or
INTELLIGENCE SUMMARY

Army Form C. 2118

(Erase heading not required.)

Place	Date	Hour	Summary of Events and Information	Remarks and references to Appendices
	28.6.16		Shrapnel wound - a premature from one of our 18-pdr Batteries. The bad weather which has been experienced the last few days still continues. A slow bombardment was carried out today and the rest of the time was occupied in wire cutting. "Z" F.S.H. CAIGER returned from Hospital to 369th Bty.	J.f.c.
			"Y" The Zeppelin still persists. In the afternoon information was received to the effect that 29-6-16 was to be "Y" day. A few shells fell in MAILLY-MAILLET during the course of the day - the enemy showed a little more artillery activity.	J.f.c.
	29.6.16		"Z" The weather cleared up today. The wire cutting and special bombardments by each Battery continued; from 4 to 5.20 p.m. an intensive Bombardment by all the Artillery was carried out. There has been a little trouble caused by the springs of 18 pdr guns breaking. Three men of Z 29 T.M. Bty were killed; the gun pit was blown up and the gun and detachment disappeared.	J.f.c.
	30.6.16		Y2. The intensive Bombardment took place today between 8 and 9.15 am. The enemy put a few shells into MAILLY and BEAUSSART.	J.f.c.

WAR DIARY
or
INTELLIGENCE SUMMARY
(Erase heading not required.)

Army Form C. 2118

Place	Date	Hour	Summary of Events and Information	Remarks and references to Appendices
			During the past week all batteries of the bty be have been engaged in wire cutting. D/130 & 379 have been particularly successful and have removed all the wire allotted to them. 369 & 370 have succeeded in cutting lanes through the wire which forms their target. [signature] 10/10/1922 Cmg/122 Bde RFA	

29th Division.

132nd HOWITZER BRIGADE

R. F. A.

JULY 1916

WAR DIARY
OF
132nd Bde R.F.A.
from 1st to 31st July 1916.

INTELLIGENCE SUMMARY

(Erase heading not required.)

Summaries are contained in F.S. Regs. Part II. and the Staff Manual respectively. Title Pages will be prepared in manuscript.

Place	Date July	Hour	Summary of Events and Information	Remarks and references to Appendices
MAILLY-MAILLET	1.		After an intense preliminary bombardment at 0720 a mine was sprung before HAWTHORNE REDOUBT and at 0730 our Infantry attacked — owing to the enemy's machine guns this did not meet with the success anticipated. All day long a very fierce struggle went on, but the 29th Division were unable to retain hold of the German Line — in the late evening the 48th Division on the Left and the 36th on the Right who had got some headway fell back to their original positions.	T.J.C.
	2.		On the night there was a great deal of fighting in the THIEPVAL Ridge about which it was difficult to derive any trustworthy information. During the course of the day orders came relating to an attack to be launched on the 29th Div. sector by the 48th 48th Div. Infantry, but later in the evening these were cancelled. Col. SMITH, D.S.O. and all the Artillery Liaison officers returned safely from the operations of July 1st. About 5.30 p.m. to 6 p.m. the Germans put about 30 "13 cm" shells into MAILLY-MAILLET In the evening about 9.45, an alarm of gas was received; this turned out to be Lachrymatory gas shells only.	J.J.C.
	3.		The 48th Division were to have attacked BEAUMONT HAMEL today, but owing to events on the night the programme was changed — severe fighting about THIEPVAL Ridge has been	J.J.C.

INTELLIGENCE SUMMARY.
(Erase heading not required.)

Summaries are contained in F.S. Regs., Part II. Title Pages and the Staff Manual respectively. Title Pages will be prepared in manuscript.

Place	Date	Hour	Summary of Events and Information	Remarks and references to Appendices
	4.		Things were fairly quiet on this portion of the line today — the enemy shelled MAILLY-MAILLET and ENGLEBELMER in a desultory fashion.	J.C.
	5.		The weather broke down badly and there was over six hours continuous heavy rain. Orders were received today re. the move of the Battery wagon lines from LOUVENCOURT. D/132 moved from their position in the MESNIL Valley to Q.34.a.	J.C.
	6.		Headquarters of the Brigade moved to ENGLEBELMER. The Wagon lines of the Batteries moved, 369 and 370 to MAILLY Wood and S 371 and D/132 to ENGLEBELMER Wood.	J.C.
	7.		4.C.W.D. EAST R.F.A. joined the Brigade and was posted to D/132. Headquarters of the Brigade moved to P.23.c.0.7. The very wet weather still continued. A successful attack was made by our troops on OVILLERS-LA-BOISELLE.	J.C.
	8.		The weather cleared up a bit. Things were pretty quiet on the front opposite this portion of the line.	J.C.
	9.		A big improvement in the weather took place. All afternoon and evening the sounds of very heavy firing to the South were heard.	J.C.

INTELLIGENCE SUMMARY

(Erase heading not required.)

Summaries are contained in F. S. Regs., Part II. and the Staff Manual respectively. Title Pages will be prepared in manuscript.

Place	Date	Hour	Summary of Events and Information	Remarks and references to Appendices
	10.		H.A.C. Bde carried out a Reconnaissance this morning for Battery positions for the defence of certain lines in the event of the enemy making a counter-attack in force.	J.f.C.
	11.		This day has been a very quiet day on our front: very little firing taking place. Situation continues to be cold & still.	J.B.C
	12.		Englebelmer has been left alone for the last 3 or 4 days, not having been shelled at all by hostiles.	J.B.C.
	13.		Col. Hankmore relinquishes Command of the Right Group on his becoming Brigadier-General. The Right Group has today been taken over by Lt. Col. Johan H Smith DSO while Major Sterbroke takes over command of 17 P.T.Bde vice Col. Hankmore ; D/132 Btty now commanded by Lt. Gray. Headquarters have moved to P24 D.	J.B.C.Y.
	14.		2/Lt Ratsey of 17 P.T.Bde R.F.A. has been temporarily attached to the Bde. About up-to 20 enemy four-five shells landed in Englebelmer, otherwise everything was fairly quiet in this part of the front.	J.B.C.
	15.		Except for occasional 4.1 hr forward ments, there is nothing of importance to report. 2/Lts 9.C. Jolant + JW. Horner arrived from the Base & were posted to 371 + 373 + 375 respectively.	J.B.C.
	16.		Around from the P.M Reserve Army — Two cars reported to say that no lights are to be shown at night as Zeppelin raids are expected.	J.B.C.

INTELLIGENCE SUMMARY

(Erase heading not required.)

Instructions regarding the _____
Summaries are contained in F.S. Regs., Part II.
and the Staff Manual respectively. Title Pages
will be prepared in manuscript.

Place	Date	Hour	Summary of Events and Information	Remarks and references to Appendices
	17.		The weather continues very wet. A raid on Enemy trenches took place during the night undertaken by 2 officers & a Cpl. who successfully bombed some Germans in their dug-outs. Gylckelmen was shelled with 150 m.m. shells about 10 P.M.	Apx. 1.
	18.		Gylckelmen was again shelled at 04 A.M. this morning for about 1/2 hr. Raining again practically all day.	Apx. 1.
	19.		Any improvement in the weather. The day was comparatively quiet on the front. During the night there appears to be a heavy bombardment taken place South of this front.	Apx. y.
	20.		The weather keeps fine the very much. Gylckelmen was shelled off and on for about 1 hr.	Apx. 7.
	21.		Except for desultory firing there is nothing of importance to report. Observation by balloon has been practically impossible owing to the misty atmosphere.	Apx. J.
	22.		Mainly nailed was shelled pretty heavily towards evening. Major Duck - Wilson of Y Bty R.H.A. was killed by a 5.9 which landed near his dug-out, could it is	Apx. J.
	23.		The bombardment of Bezières prefacing an attack by Australians here. The enemy shelled our front line trenches very distinctly heard during the night, having special attention to the new trench running from Q 17 A to Q 17 D. Retaliation by the Artillery was given with effect	Apx. J.

INTELLIGENCE SUMMARY

(Erase heading not required.)

Place	Date	Hour	Summary of Events and Information	Remarks and references to Appendices
	24.		Major Courage, 340th Bty, has taken over command of 147th Bde, vice Col. Forman who assumes command of 15th Bde, vice Col. Archdale DSO who has left to assume command of 2nd Cavalry Division Hausar. Lt. Staveley of 460th Bty has taken over command of 340th Bty; while Lt. Brett Squire ADC to Gen. Malcolm Peake has been posted to " " " while 2nd Lt. Goldie 369th Bty. goes as A.D.C. to B.G.R.A.	A409.
	25.		The 29th Division Infantry is being relieved to-night by 25th Division Infantry. The 29th Division Artillery is not being relieved.	A13.Y.
	26.		An extra Group has now been inaugurated. v13; Centre Group, now under command of Col. Marriott-Smith. The Right Group being taken over by Col. N.H.C. Sherbrooke, while the Left Group remains under command of Col. Forman.	A.A.Y.
	27.		Owing to the weather having greatly cleared up there was considerable aeroplane activity today. Three hostile aeroplanes were over our lines while four or five more came over about 7 P.M. Early in the afternoon. flying v. high.	A409.

INTELLIGENCE SUMMARY

(Erase heading not required.)

Summaries are contained in F. S. Regs., Part II. and the Staff Manual respectively. Title Pages will be prepared in manuscript.

Place	Date	Hour	Summary of Events and Information	Remarks and references to Appendices
	28		The usual routine duty took place. Enemy activity was slight. During the night our front line trenches south of Y Ravine were shelled, and our artillery were asked to retaliate. This was done.	J4og
	29		The weather continues fine every day. Several aeroplanes flew over Englebelmer in the afternoon & drawn at a great height.	J4og I
	30		A quiet day all along this sector.	J4og Y
	31		With some activity on the front of the line. Englebelmer was shelled about 12 mid night. Several shells falling in towards of Centre Group HQ. No damage was done.	J4og

L.Col R.F.A.
Comdg. 132nd Bde. R.F.A.

1/8/16

29th Division.

132nd HOWITZER BRIGADE

R. F. A.

AUGUST 1916

Army Form C. 2118

WAR DIARY
or
INTELLIGENCE SUMMARY
(Erase heading not required.)

Vol 6

WAR DIARY
of
132nd Bde. R.F.A.

from 1st – 31st August
1916.

Army Form C. 2118

WAR DIARY
or
INTELLIGENCE SUMMARY
(Erase heading not required.)

Instructions regarding War Diaries and Intelligence Summaries are contained in F. S. Regs., Part II. and the Staff Manual respectively. Title Pages will be prepared in manuscript.

August

Place	Date	Hour	Summary of Events and Information	Remarks and references to Appendices
ENGLEBELMER	1.		Comparatively quiet during the day; in the late evening the orchard where HdQrs are situated has a few shells dropped round it, but no damage was done.	T.J.C.
	2.		The enemy was more active than usual on our trenches in the morning and during the night he bombarded our front line with shells of all calibres and minenwerfer.	T.J.C.
	3.		This forenoon 370-y371 St Batteries were heavily shelled by 4-inch guns and 5.9 inch howitzers from direction of MIRAUMONT: for over two hours a very heavy fire was kept up on these Batteries but the damage done was exceptionally little - one gun pit and one ammunition pit dug out in the latter and one gun pit and dug out in the former were damaged in 371 (two severely) and one in 370 y B154 a Bdn. The casualties were three men wounded while repairing the line under heavy fire. WALKER, who was hit	T.J.C.
	4.		The enemy artillery was quiet today. From 2103 to 2106 and 2110 to 2113 we fired on selected targets near the enemy front line; the German reply to these bursts was feeble.	T.J.C.
	5.		As the 4.5" Ammunition allowance has been increased, the howitzer battery has been engaged in wire cutting. At 1540 8 Rounds gun fire were shot at the trench beside BEAUCOURT ROAD. As the enemy artillery were active on our line beside MARY REDAN the Centre Group fired 100 Rounds in Retaliation.	T.J.C.
	6.		Another quiet day.	

Army Form C. 2118

WAR DIARY
or
INTELLIGENCE SUMMARY
(Erase heading not required.)

Instructions regarding War Diaries and Intelligence Summaries are contained in F.S. Regs., Part II. and the Staff Manual respectively. Title Pages will be prepared in manuscript.

Place	Date	Hour	Summary of Events and Information	Remarks and references to Appendices
	7th		The weather continues very hot & fine. Nothing of importance to report.	JAB J
	8th		In the morning an intense bombardment took place by our Artillery of Y Ravine & Station Alley from 04.05 to 04.35.	JAB J
	9th		The enemy bombarded our trenches heavily in the afternoon in the vicinity of Broadway, the O.P. there being damaged.	JAB J
	10th		The day was dull and with a good deal of rain during the night of 9th/10th. Hows were shelled vigorously from 10 mks with 77mm shells, no damage being done.	JAB J
	11th		The weather has again cleared and very hot. During the night 11th/12th the 91st Infantry Bde was relieved by the Guards Division. Our trenches were heavily shelled during the night, Artillery retaliation being given.	JAB J
	12th		A comparatively quiet day on the front.	JAB J
	13th		At 15.00 p.m. an intense bombardment took place of a line of supposed German dug-outs. 10 mks & stokes shells reached one of their guns being smashed and one officer wounded.	JAB J
	14th		The weather has changed again and is now very dull & wet. The usual bombardment took place this afternoon at 15.30 by Trench & Artillery. A short bombardment at 02.30 (night) and	JAB J
	15th		We bombarded the German front line support trenches. There was to have been a gas attack, but the wind being unfavourable it was postponed.	JAB J

WAR DIARY
or
INTELLIGENCE SUMMARY
(Erase heading not required.)

Army Form C. 2118

Date	Hour	Summary of Events and Information	Remarks and references to Appendices
16		The gas attack, undertaken by dead daylight, that was to have taken place last night but was put off owing to unfavourable wind, had to be abandoned again to-day for the same reason.	JH37
17		Nothing of importance to report.	JH37
18		The weather does'nt shew any signs of clearing & is still dull & lowering, tho' there has been no heavy rain. Beyond the usual routine firing there has been little activity on this front.	JH37
19		Our Artillery were engaged in wire cutting & cutting lanes tho' wire & for assault. 2Lt. T.B. Thompson & Signallers from 3rd Div. Arty arrived to-day. They Div. Arty is said to be coming into action shortly on this front.	JH37
20		D/132 had a premature at one of their guns to-day. 2Lt Morrice was wounded, one N.C.O. was killed & four other gunners seriously wounded.	
21		The weather has greatly improved to-day, has seen glorious sun. At 23.00 a raid took place on the German trenches at two different points. The party which went in at the Nac at Y Ravine advanced too far to the left & got caught in our barrage fire, their officer being killed. The other party	

WAR DIARY
or
INTELLIGENCE SUMMARY
(Erase heading not required.)

Army Form C. 2118

Date	Hour	Summary of Events and Information	Remarks and references to Appendices
22.		Encountered an enemy patrol of about 6 men, and were fired on, after which the raiding parties returned. Artillery barrage was kept up from 23.00 – 23.25.	JMSJ
23.		From 09.30 – 10.30 Eyeletcher village was shelled continuously with 77mm shells. A German aeroplane came over Eyeletcher at 09.30. This morning flying very high. 390th & 391st Bty were shelled continuously the whole morning with 77 & 5.9 shells. 391st Bty had one man killed & 4 wounded, while 390/735 had one man wounded. Considerable damage was done to the gunpits, while 390 Bty had one of their guns put out of action.	JMSJ
24.		Nothing of importance to report. The weather has changed again, & is now dull showery making observation difficult.	JMSJ
25.		One of our captive balloons got lose the day before yesterday & drifted over into German lines landing at Irles. The two occupants – one of which was said to be Basil Hallam the actor – were both killed descending by parachute. 2Lt's Bostir & Hart arrived from Bag & were posted to 371 & D/135 respectively.	JMSJ

WAR DIARY
or
INTELLIGENCE SUMMARY

Army Form C. 2118

Date	Hour	Summary of Events and Information	Remarks and references to Appendices
26.		Another wet day. Derelict Junction was shelled heavily in the morning by 5-9" shells. The O.P. there being blown in.	J₁₁₃.J
27.		Raining practically the whole day. Representatives of the 39th & 49th Divisional Artillery have been selecting Battery positions preparatory to coming into the line. Instructions have been issued from 29 D.A. with reference to a test assault on the German position & various bombardments that are to take place before Zero day.	J₁₁₃.J
28.		Slight improvement in the weather. Wire cutting is being proceeded with & unknown/undisclosed registration by new batteries.	J₁₁₃.J
29.		There was a trial bombardment at 15.00 this afternoon. X-2 day. The weather continues unfavourable and is greatly hampering operations.	J₁₁₃.J
30.		X-1 day. There was another bombardment at 08.00 this morning. Observation of wire cutting has been practically impossible owing to continual rain. There have been very strong N.E. winds & heavy rain all day. Owing to unfavourable weather conditions and the consequent sodden condition of the trenches & surrounding country Zero day has been postponed 24 hrs.	J₁₁₃.J

WAR DIARY or INTELLIGENCE SUMMARY

Army Form C. 2118

Place	Date	Hour	Summary of Events and Information	Remarks and references to Appendices
	31		The Bde has now been continuously engaged night & day since 25 June. 36q Bty has had 2 guns destroyed - 370 Bty 1 gun & 371 gun & D/132 1 howitzer. Casualties all up 49. Officers wounded 3. Other ranks 25. Killed 5. Enemy fired about 5000 a gun. Time actually engaged 1760 hrs day & 1320 hrs night (approx). 6q group - 1 night. Attacks again postponed. Maricourt. Sept Monday. 37 RGA, RHA awarded Military Medal. Bde HQrs now in tactical control of XV Bde RHA. 97, 368, 369, 460 & D/147 Batteries.	

Signed I Gabriel Lt Col
R.F.A.
Comdg 152nd Bde. R.F.A.

29th Division.

132nd HOWITZER BRIGADE

R. F. A.

SEPTEMBER 1 9 1 6

Brigade was broken up 12.9.16

29th Division No. A/723

D.A.G.,
   3rd Echelon,
      BASE.

     In continuation of my No. A/723 dated 11th instant, I forward herewith War Diary for the 132nd Brigade R.F.A. for the month of September 1916.

     Please acknowledge receipt.

25th November 1916.

                    Major General,
            Commanding 29th Division.

WAR DIARY
or
INTELLIGENCE SUMMARY

Army Form C. 2118

WAR DIARY
of
132nd Bde R.F.A.

Sept 1st – 30th 1916.

Volume No. 14

Army Form C. 2118

WAR DIARY or INTELLIGENCE SUMMARY
(Erase heading not required.)

Place	Date	Hour	Summary of Events and Information	Remarks and references to Appendices
	1.		The attack has again been postponed. It is now to take place on Sept 3rd at 05.30. Italy has declared war on Germany. Roumania has declared war on Germany also. Neuestatter is still unsettled.	JHJ
	2.		Left Group H.Q's were moved forward to a position in the Mesnil Valley in preparation for to-morrow's operations. Neuestatter has cleared & promises fine for to-morrow. 2/Lt. Deane 390 Bty returns from England & rejoined his Bty. 2/Lt. Oppenheim arrived from 2nd Div. & was posted to 370 Bty. D/149 & 46th Batteries have been issued with incendiary shells which are to be fired into Grandcourt to-day &to-morrow.	JHJ
	3.		An intense bombardment on the German front & support line started at 5.10 hour & lasted this for 14 minutes after which the first wave of infantry crossed no-man's-land to the attack, the object being the capture of the German front & second lines. The barrage then lifted for a slower rate of fire by the artillery was ordered. It was not until 06.00 that the Left Group Commander received any definite information how the attack had progressed. The information received was that the Hants Regt.	

WAR DIARY
or
INTELLIGENCE SUMMARY
(Erase heading not required.)

Place	Date	Hour	Summary of Events and Information	Remarks and references to Appendices
			had reached the German front line, but had been compelled to retire owing to hostile artillery & machine gun enfilade fire. When the first wave of infantry crossed to the attack, it was impossible, owing to insufficient daylight, to see a at 4 to B.P. (Prospect Row) how things were going, and the non-arrival of any information till 06:00 from the Liaison Officer caused great inconvenience. Artillery fire was kept up till about 11:00 when it was found that the objectives had not been but attained. Fire ceased. Retaliation by the enemy was not very great. Somewhat could be seen of the attack. Our casualties do not appear to have been very heavy. Wounded could be seen crawling back to their own lines the whole afternoon. Several badly wounded were brought in after dark. Orders have been received that the 29th Div. Artillery will be concentrated ready to leave L area on Sept. 8th withdrawing from action on nights 5/6th & 6/7th. A short bombardment of the German second & third lines took place by our artillery this morning at 10:00. Shells were seen going up from the German trenches in expectation of another attack. A considerable amount of	N1734
	3.4			

WAR DIARY
or
INTELLIGENCE SUMMARY
(Erase heading not required.)

Army Form C. 2118

Place	Date	Hour	Summary of Events and Information	Remarks and references to Appendices
	5.		Lachrymatory & gas shells were fired into Mesnil Valley during the early hours of the morning & part of the preceding afternoon & night. There has been a good deal of rain. The weather is cold & unsettled.	J.B.J.
			A bombardment of the enemy's communications at 1245 and 1530 took place. The 39th Divisional Artillery took over the line at 1800 from the 29th Divl Arty: accordingly this evening 369th and D/132 Batteries pulled out of their positions to their waggon lines preparatory to moving away. There was a continuation of the bad weather.	T.J.C.
	6.		At 1200 369th and D/132 Batteries marched off to FAMECHON where they billeted for the night along with Headquarters 147 Bde. R.F.A. and 10th and 97th Batteries. Capt. C. ARMSTRONG A.V.C. was admitted to Field Ambulance with a sprained ankle owing to his horse falling on him.	T.J.C.
	7.		From 0000 to about 0400 the enemy were active in the orchards at the E. end of ENGLEBELMER with lachrymatory gas shell and a few 5.9" H.E., but no damage appears to be caused. At 0900 Headquarters, 370th and 371st Batteries marched out to FAMECHON, where they joined the other two batteries of the Brigade and took up the billets vacated by 147th Bde.	J.J.C.

1875 Wt. W503/826 1,000,000 4/15 J.B.C. & A. A.D.S.S./Forms/C. 2118.

WAR DIARY
or
INTELLIGENCE SUMMARY
(Erase heading not required.)

Army Form C. 2118

Place	Date	Hour	Summary of Events and Information	Remarks and references to Appendices
	8.9.16		Starting at 0900 the Brigade marched to BOUBERS-sur-CANCHE; as the billets were a long distance from the horse lines (most of them bivouaced)	T.J.C.
	9.		The march today was to HESTRUS, the Brigade leaving at 0900 and arriving about 1415. The watering question was rather difficult here as there was no stream within two miles and the wells in the village were very deep.	T.J.C.
	10.		Leaving at 0830 the Brigade moved to MAMETZ, arriving about 1330. The road was not so hilly today as it had been on the previous days' marches. This evening the orders concerning the re-organization of the 29th Divisional Artillery were received. The 132nd Bde was to cease to exist at 0600 on 12.9.16, Headquarters being attached to 17th Bde R.F.A., whilst Lt.Col H.R.W. MARRIOTT SMITH, D.S.O was to command, and the Batteries split up amongst the other Brigades of the Division.	T.J.C.
	11.		OCHTEZEELE was the destination today. After arrival in billets the units were very busy in getting ready to transfer to their new Brigades. In the course of the evening the Officer Commanding went round the Batteries and bade farewell to the 371 Batty, who were accompanying fire from the new Brigade	T.J.C.
	12.		Throughout the whole march the weather has been of the best. In the morning the sections of Batteries marched out to join their new units as follows:	

WAR DIARY
or
INTELLIGENCE SUMMARY
(Erase heading not required.)

Army Form C. 2118

Place	Date	Hour	Summary of Events and Information	Remarks and references to Appendices
	12 (cont.)		369th Battery — Right Section — 92nd Bty R.F.A.	
			Left Section — "Y" R.H.A.	
			370th Battery — Right Section — 26th Bty R.F.A.	
			Left Section — 13th Bty R.F.A.	
			371st Battery — Right Section — "B" R.H.A.	
			Left Section — "L" R.H.A.	
			II/132 to 17th Bde R.F.A. and to be re-named II/17 P.F.A.	
			The result of this re-organization was to give the 29th Divisional Artillery the following composition: — 2 Brigades, each with 3 6-gun 18-pdr Batteries and 14.5" (Howitzer) Battery of 4 howitzers and 1 Brigade with 2 6-gun 18-pdr Batteries and 14.5" (Howitzer) Battery of 4 howitzers. The two Batteries of the old 57 (Howr) Bde R.F.A. are now II/147 and II/17 and the 460th Battery which was the third, in addition to these two, of the original 132nd Bde R.F.A. is now in the 15th Bde R.H.A.	I/C

WAR DIARY
or
INTELLIGENCE SUMMARY
(Erase heading not required.)

Army Form C. 2118

Place	Date	Hour	Summary of Events and Information	Remarks and references to Appendices
			The Officers were transferred as under:—	
			H.Q. { Lt. Col. H.R.W. MARRIOTT SMITH D.S.O., R.F.A. to 17th Bde R.F.A. (to command) Lt T.J. CUNNISON to 17th Bde R.F.A. (Adjutant.) 2Lt H.B. THOMPSON to 147th Bde R.F.A. (to be Orderly Officer)	J.J.C.
			369 { CAPT C.G. LAWSON to "Y" R.H.A. LT F.Y. BRIGHT 92 13/y R.F.A. 2LT F.H. CAIGER " " 2Lt G.N.T. LAMB "Y" R.H.A 2Lt M. LORD	
			370 { CAPT M. STAVELEY to 13 Bty R.F.A. LT B.B. SQUIRE 92nd " " 2LT A.W. STANFORD " " " 2Lt A.H. BEAVER 26th " " LT A. EPPENHEIM " " " 2LT W. HENNEY	
			391 { CAPT G.H. BAILEY, M.O. to "L" R.H.A. 2LT N.F. HEATH L 2LT M.O. HASKELL L 2LT J. BELCHER B 2LT H. FOSTER B	D/132 { CAPT T.H. GRAY Lt A.E. HAYNES 2Lt T.H. DISLEY NOWELL HYATT

WAR DIARY or INTELLIGENCE SUMMARY

Thus comes to an end this Brigade after a chequered existence of approximately two years.

Two of its original Batteries are still with the 10th Division ie Salonica and two with the 29th Division. The 3 new to me Batteries are in cooperate) with their older sisters of the 29th Division.

This reorganisation has no doubt imp[r]oved the efficiency of the 29th Div. Artillery, but the separation has been most affect[ing] without regret on the part of those who have been mixed together.

She fighting at Helles Bay, Cape Helles – and the 2 were executing Meuspon – 3 months before the Div in France and 2 months of the Battle of the Somme form links the rupture of which cannot but cause sadness in the hearts of those whose comraderships is now severed.

[signature]
Lt Col RFA
Cmdg 132 Bde RFA

www.ingramcontent.com/pod-product-compliance
Lightning Source LLC
Chambersburg PA
CBHW081243170426
43191CB00034B/2026